Study Guide on
The Book Thief
by Markus Zusak

by Ray Moore

Contents

Preface

A Study Guide is an *aid* to the close reading of a text; it is *never a substitute* for reading a text. This novel deserves to be read *reflectively*, and the aim of this guide is to facilitate such reading. It is intended for high school and university students who wish to study this novel in depth but may lack the knowledge of the political and historical background that is essential to do so.

Neither the study questions nor the graphic organizers have answers provided. This is a deliberate choice. Even 'suggested' answers would limit the exploration of the text by readers themselves which is the primary aim. I found in my classroom that students frequently came up with answers I had not even considered, and, not infrequently, that they expressed their ideas better than I could have done. The point of this Guide is to open up exploration of the text *not* to close it down by providing 'already made answers.' Teachers *do not need* their own set of answers in order to evaluate their students' responses.

Spoiler alert!

If you are reading the novel for the first time, you may wish to go straight to the Commentary and Study Questions and come back to these sections later.

Acknowledgements:

As always, I am indebted to the work of reviewers and critics. Where I am conscious of having taken an idea or a phrase from a particular author, I cite the source in the text: failure to do so is an omission which I will immediately correct if it is drawn to my attention.

I believe that all quotations used in the book fall under the definition of 'fair use'. Once again, if I am in error on any quotation, I will immediately remove it if it is drawn to my attention.

Introduction

Plot Summary:

At the age of nine, in 1939, their mother arranges for Liesel Meminger and Werner (her six-year-old brother) to be placed with foster parents, Hans and Rosa Hubermann, who live in the small town of Molching in Germany. Unfortunately, before they can reach Molching, Werner dies, leaving Liesel traumatized. She experiences nightmares and occasional bed-wetting for months, but her foster father, Hans, is a gentle and patient man who is selflessly comforting and reassuring. His wife, Rosa, appears to be very different, impatient, brutal and foul-mouthed, but Liesel soon understands that, in her way, Rosa loves her very much. Hans helps Liesel learn to read, starting with a book Liesel stole from the cemetery when her brother was being buried.

Liesel's inability to read is humiliating when she starts school, but she is befriended by the son of a neighbor, Rudy, who does everything he can to protect her. Eventually, Liesel realizes that her father was persecuted by the Nazis for being a Communist, and that her mother was likely arrested (perhaps murdered) for the same crime. At a Nazi book-burning ceremony, Liesel salvages a book from the bonfire but is seen by the mayor's wife, Ilsa Hermann. Far from being arrested, the mayor's wife invites Liesel into her library and encourages her to browse through the books.

Because Hans once made a promise to a Jewish friend who had saved his life, he hides the man's son, Max Vandenberg, in his basement. Liesel helps to nurse Max back to health, and to repay her Max writes Liesel two stories about their friendship and about the power of words. After Hans publicly gives bread to an old man who is among a group of Jewish prisoners being marched through Molching to the concentration camp at Dachau, Max has to leave. As his punishment, Hans is drafted into the military and works in a unit given the task of minimizing damage from air raids at a time when Allied air raids over major German cities are escalating dramatically.

Faced with the fanaticism of Hitler and the increasing inevitability of German defeat, Liesel comes close to losing hope in the ability of words to influence people to behave virtuously. Two things restore Liesel's faith: first, Max leaves her a story called *The Word Shaker*, and second Ilsa gives her a blank book and encourages her to write. Every night in the basement, Liesel writes the story of her life which actually saves her life when Himmel Street is bombed out of existence and she is the sole survivor. Liesel goes on to marry, have children and grandchildren; she dies at an old age.

Why Read this Book?

Zusak, whose background is in writing novels for Young Adults, has said that he did not have a particular audience in mind when he wrote this novel. *The Book Thief* (published 2005) was on *The New York Times* Best Seller list for 375 weeks. The novel gets 4.5 stars (out of five) on amazon.com and 4.4 stars on goodreads.com. It was made into a successful movie and shows every sign of being popular for some time.

Important: Issues with this Book:

There is no sex in this book and no graphic violence. Nevertheless, the story does contain a great many deaths and, since it is narrated by Death, there is a great deal of emphasis on what may be a disturbing subject. The bombing raid that kills virtually everyone in Himmel Street is particularly sad.

Graphic organizers:

Graphic organizers are provided to enable the students to make notes. Some guidance is given which can be adapted depending on how the teacher wants them to be used.

25 July 1943: German civilians after the bombing of Hamburg.
(Image in the public domain.)

Dramatis Personæ: Selective List of Characters

Death

The narrator of the story is Death whose duty it is to carry away the souls of the dead (though it is never made entirely clear where these are taken). Of course, Death is immortal: he has been performing this task forever, and the strain is definitely beginning to tell: the capacity of humans to kill other humans is at times emotionally overwhelming. This is particularly evident since he is writing his story of the Book Thief's experiences during World War II, which massively increased the number of souls he had to collect. Initially, he encounters the Book Thief on three occasions when he arrives to take away the souls of people near to her, but the Book Thief is a survivor. Her story becomes, one of the "mere handful" of stories that illustrate the beautiful aspects of humanity, stories that, like concentrating on colors, Death uses to "distract" him/herself "as I go about my [his] work."

The Meminger family

Paula Meminger

After Liesel's father has been arrested and 'disappeared' by the Nazis for being a Communist, her mother plans to give her and her younger brother up for fostering. She contacts Frau Heinrich from the foster care agency who facilitates the placement of Liesel with the Hubermanns. Paula soon afterwards appears to suffer the same fate as her husband because all efforts by Liesel and Frau Heinrich to contact her end in failure.

Liesel Meminger

The protagonist of the story is the "Book Thief" of the title. Her story begins in January 1939 when she is "nine years old, soon to be ten." Her father, a communist, has 'disappeared' leaving her mother with two young children. Because she is often ill, the mother decides to take her children to a foster home, but on the train journey Liesel's younger brother dies. After she is placed with the Hubermanns, Liesel's mother quickly disappears (perhaps arrested or even executed by the Nazis) and all of Liesel's attempts to contact her fail. Traumatized by the loss of her family, Liesel suffers nightmares and occasionally wets the bed. Slowly, however, her stepfather, Hans, gains her trust. Though she cannot read when she comes to live with them, Liesel learns to love books, and because the family is very poor, she ends up stealing them. Paradoxically, Liesel has a very highly developed sense of fairness, compassion and morality.

Werner Meminger

Liesel's brother is only six years old when she watches him die, following a coughing fit, in a railway carriage as their mother takes them to their foster home. Liesel is haunted by the memory of his death.

The Hubermann family

Hans Hubermann (Papa)

Liesel's foster father is a skilled house painter, handyman, and occasional accordion player in the town of Molching on the outskirts of Munich. Hans is henpecked by his wife, Rosa, because of his poor education (though Rosa's was poorer) and his inability to earn enough money for them to live on. He was a soldier in World War I, though he honestly puts his survival down to cowardice. He is unfailingly generous, caring and patient, and he soon develops a close and loving relationship with Liesel, always encouraging and reassuring her. More than this, he is a good man, and he passes on his values to Liesel. Horrified by the Nazis' persecution of the Jews, he draws condemnation on himself by painting over anti-Semitic slurs on Jewish-owned homes and businesses, and he stands out against joining the Nazi Party until he has no alternative. When he discovers Liesel's burning desire to be able to read, he sets out to help her with secret midnight lessons and afternoon lessons by the Amper River despite the fact that his own reading is pretty basic. Together, the two help each other. Hans' empathy for those in pain or trouble, and his determination to keep the promise that he gave to his old army friend Erik Vandenburg cause him to place both himself and his family in danger from the Nazi regime that he detests.

Rosa Hubermann (Mama)

Liesel's foster mother has a reputation for having straightened out her previous foster children. She is abrasive, sharp-tongued, quick tempered and often vulgar in her language. A small, squat woman, she appears continually to be displeased with someone or something – often her husband or Liesel. To supplement the household income, she takes in washing and ironing for five of the wealthier citizens of Molching. Despite her harsh words and treatment of Hans and Liesel, she cares very much for them, and she has no hesitation in sheltering Max. Death describes Rosa as a good woman in a crisis.

Hans Hubermann, Junior

Rosa's and Hans's adult son is unswervingly loyal to Hitler and the Nazi regime. As a result, he and his father argue a lot about politics. One day, he calls his father a "coward" and walks out of the family home never to return. He is last heard of still alive at Stalingrad, but his fate is never given.

Trudy Hubermann

Rosa and Hans's grown-up daughter is a governess in a rich family. She appears infrequently in the novel, but speaks kindly to Liesel. Her parents do not trust her with the secret that they are hiding a Jew.

People linked to Hans Hubermann by World War I and II

Erik Vandenburg

This German Jew became Hans' closest friend during World War I when they served in the same unit. It was Erik who taught Hans to play the accordion, and he also saved Hans' life by volunteering him for letter-writing on the day the rest of their unit (including Erik) was wiped out. From Erik, Hans inherited his accordion and a tremendous sense of obligation – which is one reason he cannot hate Jews.

Max Vandenburg

Forced to flee from his home by the Nazi regime, Max eventually takes refuge in the Hubermann's basement. Max is twenty-three years old and a fighter – literally a fist fighter – but several times he comes close to giving up on life. Max feels a terrible sense of guilt over leaving his family to save himself; like Liesel he suffers frightening nightmares. During his stay at the Hubermanns' house, he befriends Liesel because of their shared love for reading and writing. He helps Liesel to develop as a writer and reader.

Walter Kugler

Max's "friend from childhood," Walter, is not Jewish but hides Max when he knows that the Nazis are after him. Walter is only just able to arrange for Max to leave Stuttgart before he is called up into the German army by finding Hans Hubermann and asking if he will keep his promise to Walter's father.

Reinhold Zucker

He is a twenty-four-year-old member of the Air Raid Special Unit in which Hans serves. Because of an argument over cards, he insists that Hans switch seats with him in their truck; when the truck has a flat tire and rolls over, Reinhold is the only one killed.

Neighbors, friends and acquaintances in the town of Molching

Alex and Barbara Steiner

Rudy's father, Alex, owns a tailor shop. He is not a supporter of the Nazi Party, but he goes along with its rules in order to protect his family. However, Alex and Barbara refuse to allow their son to be recruited into an elite Nazi training school. As a result, Rudy is still living in Himmel Street when it is destroyed in a bombing raid. At the end of the book, Alex is filled with remorse for having survived since his wife and all of his children are dead.

Rudy Steiner

The son of the Hubermanns' neighbor, Rudy has five brothers and sisters. He is only a little older than Liesel and the two form a deep bond of friendship almost from the moment they meet. Actually, Rudy is in love with Liesel, and is always trying to get her to kiss him – something that Liesel finds difficult to understand and constantly refuses. As one of six children, Rudy is always hungry. During the 1936 Berlin Olympics, Rudy colored himself black all over with charcoal one night and ran one hundred meters at the local sports field as his hero Jesse Owens, the African-American Sprinter. Physically and intellectually, Rudi comes close to embodying the Nazi ideal of the Aryan Master Race (blond hair, blue eyes, academically and athletically gifted), and, as a result, Nazi Party officials are keen to recruit him. Rudy, however, comes to hate Hitler and the

Nazi party for the suffering they have brought on Germany. Essentially a romantic, he can find no practical way to express his views.

Frau Holtzapfel

The Hubermanns' neighbor has feuded with Rosa for a long time, though the origin of their feud is unclear. Every day, she spits on the Hubermanns' door to show her contempt and is rude to Liesel. She has two sons, both of whom serve on the Russian front. Having heard Liesel read in the bomb shelter, she pays her (in coffee) to come to read to her because it helps her to cope with her sorrow and worry about her sons. This arrangement, the bombing raids and the deaths of her two sons leads to some reduction in her hostility towards Rosa.

Robert Holtzapfel

The elder of two brothers dies at Stalingrad having had his legs blown off.

Michael Holtzapfel

The younger of the brothers is already in the military hospital in Stalingrad when his brother is brought in seriously wounded. He watches over his brother until he dies. Injured, Michael returns home filled by guilt for having survived and for wanting to continue living. Eventually, he commits suicide.

Heinz Hermann

He is the Mayor of Molching who lives at 8 Grande Strasse, but he hardly appears in the story.

Ilsa Hermann

The wife of the Mayor employs Rosa Hubermann to do her laundry, which is how she gets to know Liesel. She has suffered severe depression for two decades due to the death of her only son, Johann, in the First World War. He died in 1918, shortly before the war ended. Ilsa sees Liesel taking the smoldering book from the ashes after the book-burning and, far from reporting her, subsequently lets Liesel visit and read books in her extensive library. Later, she leaves the window open which allows Liesel to steal more books. She also gives Liesel a blank book and encourages her to write her own story, *The Book Thief.*

Frau Diller

The owner of the candy store is a patriotic supporter of the Nazis. She refuses to serve anyone who does not give the Nazi salute and say "*heil* Hitler" upon entering her corner store which has a framed photo of Hitler hanging behind her counter.

Sister Maria

Liesel's first school teacher is very strict. She takes Liesel and other pupils into the corridor to administer a good hiding whenever she feels it to be necessary.

Schoolmates and other children

Ludwig Schmeikl

When Liesel sees every member of her class being given a reading test, she insists on taking part but finds herself unable to read from the book. In the playground, the children taunt her, particularly Ludwig. Liesel loses her temper and beats him up - badly. This action certainly enhances Liesel's reputation with her school mates, but it also earns her a good hiding from her teacher. Later, she helps Ludwig when he injures his ankle at the book burning and apologizes to him.

Tommy Müller

Liesel and Rudy's classmate suffered a serious ear infection as a child. He is rather deaf as a result and his facial muscles twitch. After beating up Ludwig, Liesel also hits Tommy, but he is so good natured that they later become friends. Rudy often has to stand up for him during Hitler Youth classes because Tommy is inept and always making mistakes. He is the worst soccer player on Himmel Street.

Arthur Burg

He is the fifteen-year-old leader of a gang of kids who steal produce from the neighboring farms. Because he likes Liesel and Rudy, he lets them join his gang. Arthur is scrupulously fair in dividing up what the gang steals, and he gives Liesel and Rudy a bag of chestnuts before leaving town.

Viktor Chemmel

Arthur's successor as leader of the gang is sadistic, domineering and cruel. He particularly dislikes Rudy whom he savagely beats and then throws Liesel's copy of *The Whistler* into the freezing Amper River. Viktor is from a rich family and steals for the excitement of it and not out of need; he admires Hitler.

Otto Sturm

He delivers farm produce from his family to the priests on his bike. Rudy puts water on the road that turns to ice so that Otto will fall off, and he and Liesel can steal his food.

Franz Deutscher

Rudy regards the leader of his Hitler Youth Division as "sadistic." He represents the worst aspects of the Nazi ideal, and he takes particular pleasure in tormenting and humiliating Rudy.

Genre

Bildungsroman

The Book Thief belongs to the literary genre *Bildungsroman* (the name is of German origin), that is a novel which traces the development and formation of the character of a young protagonist. *Bildungsroman* may be defined as a "novel of formation, novel of education, or coming-of-age story … a literary genre that focuses on the psychological and moral growth of the protagonist from youth to adulthood, and in which, therefore, character change is extremely important" (Wikipedia). In this case, Liesel enters the story as a girl on the verge of adolescence and by the end of the war she is physically and emotionally a young woman.

In the course of the novel, Liesel meets many challenges, but she emerges with a clear view of her own identity. Her encounters with books have a great impact on her psychological development, for it is only after learning to read that Liesel is able to understanding that Hitler's propaganda is the basis of his power and that his exploitation of hateful language that compels people to commit acts of cruelty is the ultimate reason why her father, her brother, and (probably) her mother are dead The first book she takes, at her brother's funeral, merely emphasizes how powerless Liesel is, for she is unable to read it. A few months later, even after her lessons with Hans, she fails to read in front of the class and is bullied by Ludwig Schmeikl; feeling powerless, she resorts to violence to assert herself. However, as Liesel's reading and her writing improve, she is able to tap into the power of language and to learn that there are words that have the power to counteract Hitler's words. In the course of about six years (1939 to 1945), Liesel has developed from an illiterate and therefore a powerless girl into an articulate speaker, skilled reader and talented writer and therefore an empowered young woman.

Historical Fiction:

If we take the term historical fiction (or historical novel) to apply to works set in a period at least twenty-five years before composition (e.g., a work such as Fennimore Cooper's *The Last of the Mohicans* which was set in 1757 and written in 1826), then *The Book Thief* certainly qualifies. Its narrative covers six years (1939 to 1945) with the Epilogue bringing the end of Liesel's story right up to the present day (though no precise date is given). The period covered by the main narrative covers the months leading up to and the entire course of The Second World War.

Setting

Liesel's story plays out in the (fictional) town of Molching on the outskirts of Munich (a real city in the south of Germany). Dachau, the first German concentration camp, was established in 1933, 10 miles northwest of Munich.

In January 1939, Liesel is brought to Molching to live with her foster parents, the Hubermanns, at 33 Himmel Street (ironically it means 'Heaven Street') which is in a poor area of the town. She lives there until the street is entirely demolished by an Allied bombing raid in October of 1943. Liesel then goes to live with the mayor and his wife Ilsa Hermann who have a house on the up-scale Grande Strasse.

Narrative Voice

This is what Markus Zusak has said about his choice of narrator:

> Well, I thought I'm writing a book about war, and there's that old adage that war and death are best friends, but once you start with that idea, then I thought, well, what if it's not quite like that? Then I thought what if death is more like thinking, well, war is like the boss at your shoulder, constantly wanting more, wanting more, wanting more, and then that gave me the idea that Death is weary, he's fatigued, and he's haunted by what he sees humans do to each other because he's on hand for all of our great miseries. ("Call Me Death: Odd Narrator of a Girl's Story" NPR)

The story is thus told by a first person narrator who is actually a character in the novel. Death has his own opinions and feelings about the things he/she describes which he shares openly with the reader. Being an immortal entity, Death is able to place Liesel's story into its historical context for though the narrator is *not* omniscient he/she has a pretty encyclopedic knowledge of The Second World War (so that, for example, he/she can describe the fate of the Jews in the extermination camps and of the German soldiers surrounded at Stalingrad). This is necessary because Liesel's own understanding of the war is limited by her youth and by her geographical location: she sees things as a child and only in so far as her immediate friends and acquaintances are affected.

Except for those occasions where Death addresses the reader directly (these occur particularly, but not exclusively, in the Prologue and the opening chapters of each Part), the narrator tells Liesel's story in the third person, but he is clearly *not* an omniscient narrator. He bases his narrative on the three times that he actually saw Liesel and on *The Book Thief*, the book that Liesel wrote about her life which he rescued from the wreckage of Himmel Street after it was bombed. This accounts for the fact that the narrator limits his insight into the feelings and motivations of characters; in effect, he can only state the obvious about characters other than Liesel, since he is limited by what Liesel herself understood about them. (Thus, for example, we never really find out *why* Rudy false started twice in the 100m race because Liesel never *knows* why.) Obviously the narrator can go more deeply into Liesel's feelings because he has access to her own writing, and because he feels a tremendous sense of empathy with her. This gives him a privileged insight into the protagonist's thoughts and emotions, but by no means a definitive and total understanding.

To state the obvious, Death knows everything that will happen to Liesel, and to the people with whom she comes into contact, before he/she begins writing Liesel's story. (The reader only learns in the Epilogue that the narrator is writing in either the first or second decade of the twenty-first century following the death of Liesel who has lived a long and fulfilling life.) It is an essential part of the intimate, almost confessional, relationship that Death establishes with the reader that he/she typically reveals exactly what is going to happen *before* describing *how* it came to happen. This is particularly evident in the opening chapters to each Part of the novel which tend to 'give away' what will have happened by the end of the Part. The result is that the interest of the narrative does not depend on suspense (as it does, for example, in a detective story) but on examining the often random acts that combine to lead, with terrible inevitability, to one (often tragic) outcome. This, in turn, is a reflection of the narrator's own fascination with the story: after all, Death knows the end of *every* human's story ("***HERE IS A SMALL FACT*** You are going to die."): what fascinates the narrator is *how* these ends come about and *how* humans react to them.

Themes

Human Mortality

The book is narrated by Death, whose sole job, for all eternity, is to fetch away the souls of the dead – a task which, he assures the reader, he performs fairly and gently. The experience of death is not, however, "nice," particularly for those who are left behind, and thus it takes an emotional toll on Death. Throughout the story (which spans the years immediately before the outbreak of World War II until after the surrender of Germany), the deaths of so many characters is testimony to the frailty of our hold on life. As narrator, Death emphasizes how arbitrary life is: a single decision can result (by a sequence of cause and effect quite impossible to anticipate) in one person evading death and another person rushing to meet it. Death is helpless to control such variables.

Because death seems to be so arbitrary, many characters suffer survivor's guilt because they continue to live, and continue *to want to live*, while their loved ones have died. Thus, when Michael Holtzapfel returns home from Stalingrad, where his brother died, he is overcome with guilt for having lived, and when his mother refuses to go to the basement shelter, Michael condemns himself for doing so because he still wants to live. In an example of tragic irony, Michael commits suicide because he can no longer endure the guilt he feels.

Most characters, however, eventually overcome their guilt, and they do so because of the love shown to them by others. Liesel is the obvious example. She is haunted by the image of her dead brother which comes to her in terrible nightmares. However, the unconditional love of her foster father teaches her to show love to others so that when Liesel returns to Frau Hermann's house to thank her, for the first time she feels her dead brother's approval and after that he fades from her nightmares. Similarly, Max feels tremendous guilt for running away from his family during a wave of Jewish persecution, even though everyone in the family wanted him to go because it was his last chance. It is Liesel's loving care for him both when he arrives in Himmel Street and when he is seriously ill that convinces him that his greatest responsibility to the dead is to go on living. In the same way, Liesel's shared love of books helps Frau Hermann to move past the trauma she has suffered since the death of her son in 1918.

The Human Capacity for Evil and for Good

The novel shows the paradox of human nature: Death is continually fascinated and horrified by the capacity of people for great acts of cruelty and for great acts of kindness. As he writes, "I am haunted by humans." Sometimes, it is small actions such as Frau Holtzapfel spitting on the Hubermann's door each day, or the petty vindictiveness of Viktor Chemmel and Franz Deutscher towards Rudy, and (on the other side) Liesel describing the weather each day to Max, Rudy wading into an icy river to save Liesel's book, Ilsa Hermann inviting Liesel into her library, or Rudy giving a teddy bear to the dying pilot. Such acts, however, take place in the context of the conflict between the evil perpetrated by Hitler and the Nazis and the inherent morality of several of the book's characters.

We also see far more dramatic examples of each human extreme. The Hubermanns commit a great act of kindness in hiding and caring for Max, for in doing so they risk their lives. They care for him not only physically, by providing food and shelter, but also emotionally, making him feel like a part of the human family. Liesel, in particular, cares for Max, and the two develop a strong bond. Given the political context of the time, with hatred and violence against Jews being almost universal, Max clearly finds Liesel's kindness extraordinary. At the other extreme are the extermination camps where, as Death graphically describes, Jews are murdered on an industrial scale. Nor can the ordinary citizens of Germany claim not to know what their government is doing in their name since hundreds of Jews are marched through Molching on the way to their deaths in Dachau. Individuals give vent to their anti-Semitism when they curse the Jews and when Nazi soldiers mercilessly whip Hans, Liesel and Jewish prisoners and no one steps up to save them. In this broader socio-political context, simple acts of humanity such as when Hans paints out racist graffiti on the doors of Jews or when he impulsively rushes forward to give a starving old Jew a piece of bread, become acts of political rebellion and therefore both very dangerous and very admirable.

Double Lives in Nazi Germany

The Nazi Party demands complete obedience both to its racist ideology and to the laws which enforce it. When Rudy covers himself in charcoal to emulate his hero Jesse Owens, he is too young to understand how his action will be perceived by loyal Nazis, and his father has to try to explain it to him. Similarly, when, at the book-burning, Liesel suddenly shouts out, "'I hate the *Führer* ... I *hate* him,'" Hans uncharacteristically slaps her "squarely in the face" because it is the only way he can think to bring home to her the danger of such open opposition to Hitler.

In the political climate of Nazi Germany, people who retain their humanity (e.g., people who do not hate Jews) must appear to conform in public whilst acting very differently in the privacy of their own homes. Thus, both Liesel and Rudy must not only become members of the Hitler Youth but show enthusiasm for its ideal and activities. The Hubermanns lead double lives even before they begin hiding Max in their basement, though this 'criminal' action raises the danger of their secret subversion.

The Power of Words

At the beginning of the novel, Liesel takes a book while attending her brother's funeral. She does not take it because it *is* a book, but simply because it is a memento, something that reminds her of her brother. When she is placed in school, Liesel becomes *conscious* that she is unable to read, and only with that developing consciousness comes her desire to learn to read. This she achieves due largely to her foster father, Hans, a man who is painfully aware of his own poor reading. When she first comes to live with the Hubermanns, Liesel is traumatized and virtually silent. Again, it is Hans' patience and support that helps Liesel to discover the words to express her sense of loss and so begin to come to terms with her trauma. As her story progresses, she also learns that she has the desire and the ability to express herself in writing. Hans begins this process by teaching her the correct spelling and meanings of individual words, but it is Max (a young Jew who already understands the power that compassionate, loving words have to defy the Fuhrer) who sets an example for Liesel with the two books that he writes for her. Later, it is Frau Hermann who sees in her a potential as a writer and provides her with a book in which to write her story. By the end of the story, Liesel is an able speaker, reader and writer; the development of her literacy skills parallels her physical growth and psychological development.

Liesel soon understands that language, reading, and writing have been appropriated by the upper classes (people like the mayor have libraries while people like the Hubermanns do not normally own books). More specifically, the ruling Nazi Party has used the power of the spoken and written word to generate hatred and promote aggression while seeking to eradicate the words of its opponents. Liesel's rescue of a novel from a book-burning symbolically represents her unconscious desire to reclaim intellectual freedom from Nazi control. The more mature Max fully understands that Hitler has used words to conquer the world. His painting over the pages of *Mein Kampf* and using them to write his own stories about the constructive power of words is likewise symbolic of his more conscious desire to reclaim intellectual freedom.

There are thus two different kinds of language in opposition in the novel: the dangerous power of words that can be exploited to promote and maintain tyranny, and the healing power of words to further love between humans. Liesel and Hans develop their deep bond as he teaches her to read; Liesel's descriptions of the weather outside to Max establish a bond between them; Max's gift of the two stories he writes for her show just how much he feels for her. "The Word Shaker" acknowledges the power of words and analyzes how Hitler uses words and not guns or money to take over the world. The story essentially dramatizes the way Liesel has used words to create a refuge for herself from the encompassing evil of the Nazis – a refuge in which Max is also able to find shelter. In the basement during the air raids, Liesel reads words to calm her neighbors and to give Frau Holtzapfel some comfort by reading to her. Progress is not always smooth: after seeing Max on his way to a concentration camp, Liesel despairs and rips up a book in Ilsa's library, because she has momentarily lost faith in the power of words to defeat Hitler. Ultimately, however, it is Liesel's words in the book she leaves behind after the bombing that establish the emotional connection that Death feels to her, and provides the inspiration for him to write the story of the Book Thief through which he/she creates a connection with the reader and between the reader and the characters of Liesel's story.

Stealing and Morality

The act of stealing would seem to be morally wrong, but in the novel things are not so simple. Ironically, some of the thieves in the story are amongst its most moral characters. Arthur Burg, for example, is scrupulously fair in the way he distributes the apples and vegetables that his gang steals from the surrounding orchards and farms, and though Rudy and Liesel do once rob Otto of the food he is taking to the priests, they never do so again because they recognize that what they did was wrong. Moreover, the narrator puts such actions in the context of the hunger that the children are suffering because there is not sufficient food at home. The greater theft is that of Germany's peace and prosperity which Hitler has stolen and destroyed. Similarly, many of Rudy's attempts at theft (most of which come to nothing) can be seen as motivated by his desperate need, after a string of hard defeats at the hands of Nazi bullies, to gain some victory.

The most persistent thieving in the story is obviously that of Liesel, the Book Thief, yet even this is presented in ways that justify it. The first book she takes has been dropped into the snow by the gravedigger, and the second she salvages from the bonfire after the book-burning held in celebration of Hitler's birthday – to steal such a book is a political act of protest against a totalitarian regime. The third book she takes from Ilsa Hermann's library is one that Ilsa offered to give her, and subsequent thefts are a response to the Hermanns' decision to stop using Rosa to do their laundry. These thefts, like Rudy's less successful efforts, are Liesel's attempt to reclaim some sense of power in a situation where she feels helpless. Realizing this, Ilsa becomes Liesel's co-conspirator by facilitating her thefts.

Symbols

Colors

In the Prologue, Death informs the reader that he/she always notices colors when he/she comes for a soul because colors serve to distract him from considering the human implications of what has happened, "I do, however, try to enjoy every color I see – the whole spectrum ... It takes the edge off the stress. It helps me relax." Ironically, however, Death associates the three occasions on which he encounters the young Liesel with (respectively) white, black and red which he identifies unambiguously with the Nazi flag, the Swastika. In doing so, Death implicitly blames Hitler for all of the suffering and death in the war.

Books

In the story, books are the way in which ideas are disseminated. Hitler's *Mein Kampf* has effectively popularized his ideas and his views on the future of Germany. It has generated a mass movement, fueled by hatred of 'the other', that leads to persecution of the Jews and ultimately to a world war. The Nazi ideology can only survive, however, by preventing people from reading those books which have ideas which challenge or contradict it. The Nazis therefore burn all such books, yet inevitably some books remain undestroyed, like the novel that Liesel saves from the book-burning – a novel which has as its protagonist a sympathetic Jewish character.

In *The Word Shaker*, Max explains the importance of books, and specifically the importance to him of Liesel's love of reading. He presents words as seeds, seeds that Hitler has sown to create a forest, the trees which cast down on the people their leaves, which represent those words of hatred that convince them to support the Nazi ideology. Liesel, however, grows her own tree out of her compassion for others (specifically out of the seed of the tear she shed for the Jew Max), in which she takes shelter. This tree, which overtops the other trees in the forest of hatred, produces words (leaves) of love and compassion which Liesel shakes down onto the people. The tree is indestructible so that all of Hitler's attempts to chop it down end in failure. So secure is Liesel's tree that Max is able to climb it and take shelter there with her (as he did in the basement). Even when the two leave the tree, it falls to provide them with a safe path through the forest of hatred.

Hans' Accordion

Hans's accordion originally belonged to the Jew Erik Vandenburg, the friend who saved his life. Thus, its music represents the joy that Hans feels in the life that, but for Erik, he would not have had. The accordion also represents the obligation that he feels to help Erik's family in any way that he can in order to repay the debt he owes to his old friend. Hans does not play the accordion faultlessly; he plays it the way he lives his life, with verve and energy creating happiness for those around him.

Bread

Bread is called the "staff of life" because it is a very basic food that supports life. In the novel, giving bread is an act of selflessness, and it represents the kindness of which people are capable. Both Walter Kugler and the Hubermanns bring Max bread when he is in hiding; Hans gives the starving Jewish prisoner the bread as the Jews are marched through town, and later Liesel and Rudy do the same. In each case, those who give bread have scarcely enough food for themselves, and they risk severe punishment for their acts of compassion.

Study Guide: Commentary and Questions

How to use this study guide:

The questions are not designed to test you but to help you to locate and to understand characters, settings, and themes in the text. They do not normally have simple answers, not is there always one answer. Consider a range of possibly interpretations - preferably by discussing the questions with others. Disagreement is to be encouraged!

PROLOGUE

DEATH AND CHOCOLATE

Initially, the reader is likely to find it difficult to identify the first person narrator. To identify the narrator as 'Death' solves some, but not all, of the reader's problems: it explains the narrator's claim to be omniscient (normally a quality reserved for third person narrators) and his/her ability to transcend time. What it does not explain is the narrator's character: he/she appears very human, sensitive to color and light and to the feelings of the souls that he collects. This is no stereotypical 'Grim Reaper'!

Having to die may not be "nice," but it nothing terrible either since Death "as genially as possible" carries "you gentle away." In contrast, Death finds it difficult to even look at the "leftover humans" – the people for whose souls he knows that he must someday come but who have been left behind by their contemporaries who have not survived. Their situation is tragic, and to distract himself from their sorrow, he concentrates on colors first and humans second. This leads him/her to introduce the protagonist of the story: the book thief, "one of those perpetual survivors," whom the narrator saw three times when he came to take away people close to her.

1. Death tries to look at the colors first. Explain why.

2. The narrator emerges as a character for which the reader is likely to feel sympathy. How is this achieved?

3. Why is Death motivated to tell the story of the book thief?

BESIDE THE RAILWAY LINE

The narrator describes his/her first encounter with the book thief. Each of his three encounters will be associated in his mind with a particular color that reflects the mood of the moment. The color here is white (which is strictly speaking the *absence* of color) because the death occurred on a train traveling through a winter landscape. He/she had come to collect the soul of a small boy who had died on a journey with his mother and sister. Two guards argued about what to do with the boy's dead body and the mother and daughter; one persuaded the other to get them all back on the train and take them to the next station.

Death admits to making "the most elementary of mistakes": he allowed himself to become interested in the young girl and to empathize with her fear and sorrow.

4. What appears to be the function of the portions of the narrative that appear in bold, centered print?

5. Death describes him/herself as having "made the most elementary of mistakes." Explain how the mistake is reflected in the narrator's description in the last seven lines of the chapter.

THE ECLIPSE

Flash forward several years to the second time Death encountered the book thief. The dominant color is black because the incident happened just before dawn: he/she had come to take the soul of a pilot killed in a plane crash during World War II. The girl and a boy were among the people drawn to the sight of the crash. This time it is the gesture of the boy giving the pilot a teddy bear and of the apparent smile on the pilot's face ("A final dirty joke") that 'gets to' the narrator.

6. What do you think is the significance of Death catching "an eclipse when a human dies"?

THE FLAG

The narrator describes his/her third and final encounter with the book thief. Death arrived in a German town moments before it was devastated by an Allied air raid. He still heard the echo of the children playing in the street – children whose souls he/she had come to gather. The dominant color was red – the color of the exploding sky and of the blood of the victims. Death was early, but everything else came too late to save the children. The Book Thief was not amongst the killed but she was left alone by the killing.

From a garbage truck, Death salvaged a book the girl had written her story in. It is this incident that allowed Death to tell the girl's story in what he calls "an immense leap of an attempt – to prove that you, and your human existence, are worth it."

7. What motivates Death to want to say "'I'm sorry, child'" to the Book Thief?

8. What do you think is the "septic truth [that] bleeds clarity"?

9. Why does Death take from the garbage truck? Why?

10. What is the significance of the colors red, white and black? (The clue is in the title of this chapter.)

PART ONE: the grave digger's handbook

ARRIVAL ON HIMMEL STREET

The narrator expands upon his/her first meeting with Liesel Meminger explaining her brother's death, the purpose of the journey, and her first, troubled meeting with her foster parents, Hans and Rosa Hubermann who live on Himmel Street in a town called Molching just outside Munich. Liesel's brother dies before her eyes: she is traumatized by what she sees and by the loss of her biological mother that quickly follows. Death admits to making a mistake in attending the boy's funeral at all – evidently Liesel has captured his interest and sympathy. This is the first time Liesel steals a book (in this case a copy of *The Grave Digger's Handbook*) that fell from the pocket of a young apprentice who dug her brother's grave.

Death notes that, in the case of the two guards and two grave diggers, one did as the other said. The narrator asks, "what if the *other* is a lot more than one?" This is precisely the situation in Germany where Hitler has imposed his will (disastrously) on a whole country.

11. How does Death forge a link between the boy's death and the rise to power of Adolf Hitler?

12. Why does the narrator comment that whoever named Himmel Street had "a healthy sense of irony"? How does Liesel react to her new home?

13. Foreshadowing closes the chapter? What do you infer from the final sentence?

GROWING UP A SAUMENSCH

The chapter begins with a flash forward in which the narrator surveys all of the books that Liesel came to own and asks when "the books and the words started to mean not just something but everything." The narrator explicitly introduces the political context in which the story is set. Liesel's hair is "a close enough brand of German blond," but she has brown eyes, which are considered dangerous in Nazi Germany (blue eyes being considered essential to the Aryan race of superior Germans). We learn that her father was a communist – the full implications of which the narrator (and the reader) understands much better than Liesel does.

Liesel immediately senses that her foster father, Hans, is "worth a lot." He is gentle and patient, the very opposite of his wife Rosa.

14. Explain the significance of Liesel's father having been a "Kommunist."

15. Rosa loves Liesel. Explain how the narrator makes this clear to the reader.

THE WOMAN WITH THE IRON FIST

The narrator uses an oxymoron when he/she describes "the <u>brute</u> strength of the man's <u>gentleness</u>, his *thereness*." There is nothing weak about Hans; his determination is absolute, and Liesel recognizes this. In contrast, Rosa Hubermann appears to be angry against the whole world for the poverty in which she lives. She blames her husband for not having a 'real' job that brings in a living wage, and attacks her own laundry customers for being rich and lazy. Certainly, she seems to be a tyrant to Liesel.

The chapter introduces the characters of Molching, a typical German suburb. Some of these will be significant in Liesel's story but it is not at this point clear which. (Clue: Look out particularly for the "'crazy'" woman who lives at 8 Grande Strasse.) Political context is provided when Liesel must enroll in the BDM (*Bund Deutscher Mädchen*, Band of German Girls) which meets Wednesdays and Saturdays. The girls learn to correctly perform their "*heil Hitler*" salutes, and skills like bandage rolling, sewing, and marching, and go on hikes. You can sense immediately that Hans is not enthusiastic about the BDM.

16. Why does Liesel hide *The Grave Digger's Handbook*? What, for her, does the book signify?

Explain how Hans reacts to Liesel's nightmares and occasional bedwetting.

17. Why is school a particularly difficult experience for Liesel?

18. Which of her laundry clients does Rosa detest the most? Explain why. What happens when Rosa sends Liesel to this client's door?

THE KISS (A CHILDHOOD DECISION MAKER)

This chapter describes the way in which Liesel integrates with the children of the neighborhood and particularly with her immediate neighbor Rudy Steiner. Liesel (and the reader) begin to see how the community of the town has been affected by the racial theories of the Nazi Party: the destruction of Jewish businesses, and the compulsory yellow Star of David painted on Jewish property as in Schiller Strasse "**The road of yellow stars**." Nazi supporters are represented by the candy shopkeeper, Frau Diller, who requires her customers to "*heil Hitler*" when they enter and refuses to serve them if they do not.

The chapter ends with foreshadowing. Rudy tells Liesel, "'One day ... you'll be dying to kiss me,'" but Liesel is confident that, "As long as she and Rudy Steiner lived, she would never kiss that miserable, filthy *Saukerl* ...'" The narrator knows that they will both prove to be right.

19. Explain why Rudy supports Liesel when she insists on staying in goal while he takes his penalty.

20. What aspects of Rudy Steiner's character does the "Jesse Owens" incident suggest?

THE JESSE OWENS INCIDENT

James Cleveland (Jesse) Owens (September 12, 1913 – March 31, 1980) was an American track and field athlete who won four gold medals at the Berlin Olympic Games of 1936 (100m, 200m, 4x100m Relay and Long Jump). Various myths have grown up about Hitler's reaction to the victories of a black man over the Aryans: Hitler refused to shake Owens' hand; Hitler stormed out of the stadium following an Owens victory. Neither of these things happened. (Do the research.)

Rudy is completely naïve when it comes to the realities of racism in Hitler's Germany. This is evident when his father asks him what he is doing running on the track covered in charcoal and he replies, "'I was being Jesse Owens.'... as though it was the most natural thing on earth to be doing." His father tries to use the incident to educate his son, but with very little success. Alex Steiner is a member of the Nazi Party: he cannot bring himself to hate Jews, but he puts the safety of his family before everything else. The chapter ends with foreshadowing of the future destruction of Jewish businesses.

21. Mr. Steiner's politics are complex and contradictory. How do they explain his reaction to his son's attempted emulation of Jesse Owens?

22. What is Rudy's father trying to make Rudy understand when he tells Rudy that he should be happy he was born with blonde hair and blue eyes?

THE OTHER SIDE OF SANDPAPER

The National Socialist German Workers' Party (NSDAP) was founded on February 24, 1920 and dissolved, following the defeat and surrender of Germany, on October 10, 1945. The Brownshirts (the Sturmabteilung or SA) were the paramilitary wing of the Nazi Party using violence against rival political movements and securing Adolph Hitler's rise to power in the 1920s and early 1930s. Its head was Staff Chief Ernst Röhm under whom it rose to number three million men by the end of 1933. For complex reasons, after Hitler obtained national power in January 1933, he decided that the Brownshirts represented a threat to his power, so, in June 1934, he personally instituted a purge of the organization. In what came to be called The Night of the Long Knives, Ernst Röhm and as many as two hundred other officers in the SA were shot and later publicly discredited. The Brownshirts continued to exist, but their threat to Hitler's political control of Germany had been broken.

"People have defining moments," and for Liesel it is the night that Papa finds her stolen book and discovers her great desire to read it. The first chapter of *The Grave Digger's Handbook* is about "Choosing the Right Equipment" because grave digging is a serious occupation; in a way, Liesel is beginning to gather the equipment she will need for the job of life.

23. What event leads to Liesel's bed wetting? How are the two connected?

24. Hans is a wonderful papa, but this sets a problem for the author: how to avoid sentimentality. How do you think that the author tries to avoid sentimentality in this chapter? How successful is he?

THE SMELL OF FRIENDSHIP

Dachau, the first of many concentration camps established by the Nazis, was opened in 1933 to hold political prisoners. Over time, it grew into a system of interconnected camps and was used to house forced laborers and Jews. These camps were liberated by U.S. forces on April, 29, 1945. Nearly 32,000 inmates are known to have been killed in the camp, but the total number is not known.

The married life of Hans and Rosa appears to be one long battle. They argue all of the time, and Rosa has a pretty crude way of expressing herself. Nevertheless, Hans appears to get Mama to acquiesce to his teaching Liesel to read – so long as he does it somewhere other than their kitchen. On fine afternoons, Hans begins taking Liesel to the Amper River near the "wooden-planked bridge." It is an idyllic setting, but the river is "pointing in the direction of Dachau." This seems to be the reason for a sudden change in Hans' mood.

The narrator hints that there is a story behind Papa's accordion, a "Story within story" that Liesel will learn later.

25. Liesel notices a change in Hans when they are at the river, but doesn't realize what it means. Why do you believe Hans is going to the river?

26. What elements blend together to create the "Smell of Friendship" for Liesel? Rosa tells Hans, "'You stink,'" but "Liesel loved that smell." Account for the different reactions of Liesel and Rosa.

THE HEAVYWEIGHT CHAMPION OF THE SCHOOL-YARD

On September 1, 1939, Hitler invaded Poland from the west; two days later, France and Britain, bound by treaties to protect Poland, declared war on Germany, beginning World War II. This was the last of a series of aggressive moves by Germany which had previously been met by Appeasement from the French and British governments. Perhaps Hitler felt that the Allies would once again stand back and take no action.

The power of words is the central theme of the book. Just prior to her brother's death, Liesel has a dream of listening to Hitler make a speech. We are told, "She was listening contentedly to the torrent of words spilling from his mouth." Because she lacks the power to use and control words herself, she admires Hitler's ability to manipulate language and (like so many of the German people) falls victim to his power over words. Hitler's voice over the radio motivates an entire nation to go to war. In contrast, Liesel begins Part One hardly able to speak for herself and unable to read, and she ends without having made obvious progress. That is why she resorts to violence when she is taunted.

27. Death links two events that occur in September – November 1939. What parallels do you find between the two?

28. On her way home, Liesel is overcome with emotion. Rudy is uncritically supportive of her. In what way does Liesel achieve a breakthrough in dealing with her trauma?

29. Explain the two similes used in the final sentence of this chapter to describe Liesel's future mastery of language.

PART TWO: the shoulder shrug

A GIRL MADE OF DARKNESS

The burning of books in Nazi Germany was part of Hitler's plan to keep German literature and culture pure from influences that the Nazis considered degenerate. The first mass book-burning occurred on May 10, 1933, when university students burned more than 25,000 volumes of "un-German" books. This was the beginning of state censorship and control of culture. All political parties except the National Socialists were officially banned on July 14, 1933.

The narrative flashes forward to April 20, 1940 (Hitler's birthday) when Liesel steals her second book. She is driven to steal the book by "anger and dark hatred," but what has caused those feelings we do not know. The reader also learns that her theft helps Hans figure out "a plan to help the Jewish fist fighter." This also is unexplained. In Part Two, the narrator will fill in the missing details.

30. At the time she steals her second book, the narrator describes Liesel as "a girl made of darkness." Explain the meaning of this metaphor.

THE JOY OF CIGARETTES

Finishing *The Grave Digger's Handbook* marks an important stage in Liesel's psychological recovery. She is able to share her brother's name, Werner with Hans. The two books that Liesel gets for Christmas (*Faust the Dog* by Mattheus Ottleberg and *The Lighthouse* by Ingrid Rippinstein) are fictional. The surname suffixes "-berg" and "-stein" have become associated with Jews because many Jews have them. The dog's "obscene drooling problem" parallels Liesel's own bed-wetting, but his "ability to talk" points the way toward mastery of language as a way to deal with problems.

Life with the Hubermanns is full of hardship because of their poverty, but it is also full of happiness because, though they have a strange way of showing it, Hans and Rosa love each other deeply and they both love Liesel. However, Hans and his adult son "argued about a thing she did not understand. Something called politics."

31. The last line in *The Gravedigger's Handbook* reads "We wish you every success with your career in the funerary arts and hope this book has helped in some way." How does this relate to Liesel's development?

32. Beneath the happiness of Christmas and of the unexpected gifts she is given, there are several examples of ominous foreshadowing in this chapter. Explain them.

THE TOWN WALKER

Times are getting harder, and one of Mama's customers has to cancel his laundry order. Mama gives Liesel the task of collecting and delivering the laundry in the hope that her customers will find it harder to tell her than they are cancelling their laundry. This means walking all over town, but Liesel does not mind this because it gets her out of the house and away from Rosa's complaining. Clearly Hans and Rosa know something about Liesel's mother that the young girl does not know.

33. When Mama gives Liesel her orders about delivering the laundry, Liesel expects a comforting gesture but instead Rosa holds a wooden spoon under her nose. The narrator comments, "It was a necessity as far as she [Rosa] was concerned." What does he/she mean by this?

34. Contrast Rudy's two letters to Liesel. Why does Sister Maria find the first one unacceptable?

35. Explain Liesel's reasons for wanting to write to her birth-mother.

36. Speaking of her birth-mother, Mama says, "'Who knows what they've done to her.'" Who are 'they'? What is Rosa implying about Liesel's mother?

DEAD LETTERS

The letters that Liesel writes to her real mother are "dead" because there is no chance at all that they will reach her – probably she is already dead. Even when she has mailed her remaining letters to her mother, Liesel understands that "her mother would never write back and she would never see her again." Following Rosa's beating, Liesel is in the blackest despair, but (inexplicably) she sheds a yellow tear. It is so dark in the kitchen that she could not have been able to see a yellow tear. Later, when Liesel thinks back to this moment, she remains sure that her tear was yellow. The tear symbolizes the light of consciousness within Liesel: not only is she beginning to understand the connections between Hitler and the disappearance of her parents, but she is increasingly seeing reading as an act of personal revolt against the forces of oppression.

37. What does Mama's reprimand of Papa on Liesel's birthday tell the reader about her true feelings for the girl?

38. Rosa's reaction when she discovers that Liesel has spent a little of the laundry money is complex and contradictory. Explain it. (Be sure to explain Rosa's action when she "reached down and leaked a little, 'I'm sorry, Liesel.'")

HITLER'S BIRTHDAY

April 20, 1940, was Hitler's fifty-first birthday. Earlier in the month, German forces had invaded and occupied Norway and Denmark. In May, Germany invaded Belgium, France, Luxembourg and the Netherlands. Everywhere, Hitler's policies appeared to be leading to victory.

The Battle of Stalingrad lasted from July/August, 1942 until February 2, 1943. After months of fighting, the German 6th Army, comprising a quarter of a million men, found itself encircled and cut off. Attempts to relieve the trapped German troops failed and the pocket gradually contracted. Hitler ordered the trapped 6th to fight to the last man. On the morning of February 2, 1943, General Strecker surrendered all German forces to the Soviets. German casualties amounted to 850,000 men wounded, killed or captured. This defeat not only stopped the German advance into the Soviet Union but marked a decisive turning point in war in favor of the Allies.

The reader learns that Hans' application to join the Nazi Party was rejected because he painted the houses of Jews, earning him the name "the Jew painter" and even worse because he painted over racial slurs painted on a Jewish shop front. It is surprising that Hans, who is obviously a loving father, should be on such bad terms with his son Hans Junior, but this is because his son has completely bought into the Nazi ideology.

39. Why does Hans not regard never having joined the Nazi Party as a mistake? Why does Hans Junior take the opposite view? How would you describe Hans' feelings for his son?

100 PERCENT PURE GERMAN SWEAT

Liesel marches with the Hitler Youth divisions and is taken up in the group identity forgetting "about her mother and any other problems of which she currently held ownership." The children march strictly in step. (Tommy Mueller's inability to hear leads to a disruption in the ranks of the marching Hitler Youth. This symbolically foreshadows the problems of dissent that he, Rudy and Liesel will encounter.) Despite her love of books, Liesel feels "compelled to see the thing lit. She couldn't help it." Individuality has been destroyed by 'group-think'. At the bonfire, a man in a brown shirt stands behind a podium and makes a speech, warning the crowd to protect themselves against those who are destroying Germany, particularly Jews and communists. The Party recognizes the power of words and uses its power to keep people from words and ideas that contradict those of Hitler's regime and encourage freedom of conscience. This has a big impact on Liesel who thinks of her father, mother, and brother and understands for the first time that they were killed by the Nazis. Suddenly she seeks to escape from the group hysteria of the book-burning. In doing so, she encounters her old enemy Ludwig Schmeikl in whom she identifies a fellow victim "soon to be trampled" by the group melee.

40. Explain Liesel's complex feelings about marching in the parade and the book burning. What is the significance of the mutual apology that Ludwig Schmeikl and Liesel exchange?

41. At the end of the chapter, the narrator writes, "A single word leaned against the girl." What is that word? What has Liesel come to understand about the power of that word in this chapter?

THE GATES OF THIEVERY

Liesel finally articulates who is responsible for the loss of her family and this gives her book stealing a political purpose. Banned books now represent words that she can take back from Hitler who has taken everything from her.

Hans explains to Liesel that they live in two different worlds: the private and the public. In the public world they must stifle their true feelings and play along with demands of the Nazi Party; only in private can they speak the truth.

42. How can the Führer be "the they that Hans and Rosa Hubermann were talking about that evening when she first wrote to her mother"? Explain.

43. Why does Papa slap Liesel across the face? What does his action show about how he is trying to survive in Nazi Germany? How does Liesel react to the slap?

BOOK OF FIRE

Liesel steals a book titled *The Shoulder Shrug* which, the reader later learns has a Jewish protagonist "presented in a positive light," which was why it was at the book burning. Liesel's second theft is deftly done, but she is seen. By the description, the person who saw appears to be a woman. (The attentive reader will know her identity.)

44. Comment on the narrator's metaphor, "a small section of living material slipped from inside the ash."

45. The narrator says of the witness to Liesel's theft, "If it had a face, the expression on it would have been one of injury." Explain what you think he/she means.

PART THREE: mein kampf

Mein Kampf (*My Struggle*) is an autobiography by the National Socialist leader Adolf Hitler published in 1925 (Volume 1) and 1926 (Volume 2). In it Hitler outlines his political ideology and his future plans for Germany.

THE WAY HOME

Liesel is afraid that when Hans realizes she stole another book he will be angry because theft is wrong. However, Papa is not angry, presumably because destroying books so that no one will be able to read them is much worse than taking a book because you do want to read it.

46. After Papa discovers the book that Liesel has stolen, he has a sudden idea. He keeps exclaiming, "'Of course.'" What action does he decide to take? What advantage does he hope to gain from it?

THE MAYOR'S LIBRARY

Liesel lives in dread of the mayor's wife informing on her for the theft of the book, but instead, on a subsequent visit to pick up Frau Hermann's laundry, the lady silently shows Liesel into the library in her house. Liesel smiles in "wonder" – her understanding of the range of books available has just expanded tremendously. As the wife of a high ranking local political figure, Ilsa's actions in covering up Liesel's crime are unexpected.

47. Why do you think that the Mayor's wife shows Liesel the library?

48. Explain why Liesel runs back to the Mayor's house.

ENTER THE STRUGGLER

The setting changes to Stuttgart where a Jewish man, Max, is in hiding in a dark, closed-up room. The man clearly knows Hans Hubermann's name, though he seems not to know the man himself. Evidently he wants something from Hans, something on which his very life depends.

49. What can you infer from the fact that an unnamed man brings him a forged identity card and an unnamed book? (Think about it: if you were a Jew on the run in Nazi Germany, what is the one book that you would want to be carrying? Clue: Look at the chapter title.)

50. Max repeats the word, "'Please.'" For what do you think he is begging?

THE ATTRIBUTES OF SUMMER

In Liesel's company, Ilsa finally has the courage to speak of the death of her son in 1918. Having heard of Ilsa's loss, Liesel says, "I'm sorry" (exactly what Rosa said to Liesel when her mother's failure to reply to her letters made it clear that Liesel's mother was dead). For the present, Liesel's relationship with the mayor's wife seems beneficial to them both. Up until this point, Liesel has seen herself as a powerless victim, a person with no real identity. Reading however, helps her to understand who she is. The narrator comments, "Once, words had rendered Liesel useless, but now, when she sat on the floor, with the mayor's wife at her husband's desk, she felt an innate sense of power." However, the narrator foreshadows a time when "the mayor's wife [will] let her down," but Liesel's command of language will save her from despair.

Arthur Berg is described with the oxymoron "an agreeable fifteen-year-old criminal." The reader will by now have picked up on a theme that Death repeats: the dual nature of man; that is, man's capacity for both good and evil.

51. Death describes Johann Hermann as "a young man parceled up in barbed wire, like a giant crown of thorns." Analyze the meaning of this simile.

52. Successfully stealing apples leads to other problems. What are they, and how successfully do Rudy and Liesel solve them?

THE ARYAN SHOPKEEPER

The lives of Rudy and Liesel are getting poorer, but they have great joy in each other's company and in little moments of good fortune – like sharing a single piece of candy. The final sentence of the chapter, however, shows their momentary happiness to be unsustainable for life in Nazi Germany is clearly not "wondrous."

53. Explain the title of the chapter.

THE STRUGGLER, CONTINUED

Summer has ended, and Max has finally escaped from hiding in Stuttgart. Traveling with forged papers is, however, very dangerous. The book is great cover! It also contains a mysterious key. (Only later does the reader understand that this is Hans' copy of *Mein Kampf*.)

54. Compare and/or contrast the struggle that Max is waging with the struggle referred to in the title of the book that he carries.

TRICKSTERS

Liesel and Rudy continue their petty thefts and do not feel too bad about it because they are so hungry. The narrator, however, stresses that, compared to Max, these two "have it easy ... [because] anything was better than being a Jew."

The leader of the gang of adolescent thieves, Arthur Burg, proves himself to be highly moral despite being a thief. As he says, "'We might be criminals, but we're not totally immoral.'" When Liesel and Rudy bring food stolen from Otto Sturm, he insists on sharing it with the whole gang; he, "showing his incongruous moral aptitude," decides that Otto's basket must be returned; when Rudy is caught on barbed wire and the farmer is after him with an ax, he helps Liesel to free Rudy; when he is leaving town, he gives Liesel and Rudy a dozen roasted chestnuts; and most nobly of all, Death tells us, he will hold his dead sister in his arms for hours so great is his love for her. (Justin T. Cass argues that "Arthur Burg represents a glorious depiction of Communism" because he is poor himself and redistributes stolen items equally amongst members of his gang. In support of the symbolism, Cass points out that "the boy who leads Liesel and Rudy to the gang is 'Fritz Hammer'; [and] the Soviet symbol is a hammer and sickle.")

55. Comment on the effectiveness of the narrator's phrase "the diabolic plan bore its fruit" to describe Liesel and Rudy's robbery of Otto Sturm.

56. Describe the tone in the final section of the chapter. How does the foreshadowing in the last line change that tone?

THE STRUGGLER, CONCLUDED

Max is twice a struggler: there is the struggle to avoid capture and almost inevitable death, and there is the moral struggle in which his conscience must balance his own safety against the risk to the people who help him.

57. Explain the internal conflict with which Max struggles as he approaches the door of the house where he hopes to find sanctuary – the spit-stained door of the Hubermanns on Himmel Street, number 33.

PART FOUR: the standover man

THE ACCORDIONIST (The Secret Life of Hans Hubermann)

Kristallnacht (the Night of Broken Glass) was a systematic attack on Jews throughout Germany that took place November 9 - 10, 1938. Synagogues were burned down, Jewish homes, schools and businesses were vandalized, and close to 100 Jews were killed. In the following days, 30,000 Jewish men were arrested and sent to Nazi concentration camps.

This chapter gives the backstory of Hans' service during the First World War as a twenty-two-year-old soldier, how he came to be friends with Max's father, and why Hans helps the young Jew. Erik Vandenburg actually saves Hans twice: first he nominates him for letter-writing on the day everyone else in his unit is killed and second Erik's accordion is the main reason why Hans is allowed to stay in Molching, despite his failure to hate Jews, because people like his playing. When Hans visited Erik's wife, he told her, "'if there's anything you ever need,'" so in helping Max, he is keeping the promise he made to Max's mother. More of the background to explain Hans' initial refusal to join the Nazi Party and the economic consequences of his moral stance. One thing becomes clear: Hans is certainly not a coward. (The possibility of having to hide Max has been there for months, though Hans has never told Liesel about it. However, knowing the backstory helps the reader better to understand some of Hans' earlier actions, particularly what he did and said to Liesel on the night she stole a book at the book-burning.)

Words also played a role in saving Hans' life; because he had neat handwriting, he was able to avoid battle.

58. As a result of his moral convictions, Hans makes a number of costly political mistakes during Hitler's rise to power. List them in chronological order.

A GOOD GIRL

59. Explain in detail exactly what Hans means when he tells Max that Liesel is "'a good girl.'"

60. What do you think that the "wild card" will prove to be?

A SHORT HISTORY OF THE JEWISH FIGHTER

The Nuremberg Laws were announced at the annual Nazi Party rally held in Nuremberg in 1935. These new laws embodied in legislation many of the racial theories that were basic to Nazi ideology: Jews were denied citizenship, they were prohibited from marrying or having sexual relations with persons of Aryan race, and they were deprived the right to vote.

Max is a fighter in every sense of the word. (Liesel and Max have each lost their families because of Hitler, and they are each fighters – not only with their fists.) When he sees his uncle die he is annoyed by the man's lack of fight – he just seems to give in. His extraordinary friendship with Walter Kugler is described and Walter's part in getting Max to the relative safety of Hans' house.

Max feels tremendous guilt about the danger to which he is exposing Hans by seeking his help.

61. How did Max escape capture on Kristallnacht? (Important: Who is the "Nazi. In uniform" who knocks on the door of the family apartment?) Why does he feel tremendous guilt about having survived? (Clue: He thinks of it as "his desertion, not only his escape.")

62. Who is the woman, and why is she the "wild card"?

THE WRATH OF ROSA

As is reflected in the final line in the chapter, Liesel has a great deal still to learn about her step-parents.

63. Explain why Liesel finds Rosa's reaction to Max unusual and why the reader should not.

LIESEL'S LECTURE

Hans has the difficult task of frightening Liesel just enough so that she understands the seriousness of keeping Max's presence a secret (even from Rudy) without further damaging her psychologically.

64. In what ways are Rosa's actions and reactions in this chapter apparently uncharacteristic of her?

THE SLEEPER

65. What points of similarity does Liesel find between herself and Max?

THE SWAPPING OF NIGHTMARES

It is simply not practical for Max to stay down in the basement all of the time because it is so cold down there that he would freeze to death. Inevitably, Liesel and Max come closer: both suffer the nightmares that their earlier lives have caused them. Max continues to be wracked by guilt simply because he has a strong will to survive, "To live. Living was living. The price was guilt and shame." The example of Max struggling with his own nightmares prompts Liesel to take responsibility for her own nightmares.

For her twelfth birthday, Liesel is given a book called *The Mud Men* "about a very strange father and son" by her foster parents, and Max determines to make her a book.

66. How does Rudy help Liesel to keep her sanity?

67. What comparison does Death make to Liesel reading in the Mayor's library to Max living in the basement? To put this another way, what do you understand by the sentences, "Every time she picked up or delivered from the mayor's house, she read three pages and shivered, but she could not last forever. Similarly, Max Vandenburg could not withstand the basement much longer."

68. What prompts Liesel to tell Papa "that she should be old enough now to cope on her own with the dreams [nightmares]?

PAGES FROM THE BASEMENT

Max transforms the pages of *Mien Kampf* from something hateful into something positive by replacing Hitler's story with his own. The story of a bird who is scared of men standing over him is a symbol for Max's own life. The idea for the book's symbolism was given to Max by Liesel's description of his hair as being "'like feathers.'" In the end, the 'standover man' turns out not to be a man at all but a young girl.

69. With close reference to Max's graphic novel, explain how the concept of a 'standover man' has changed for him.

PART FIVE: the whistler

THE FLOATING BOOK (Part I)

As he/she often does, Death skips ahead in the story's timeline, but on this occasion he/she does so twice. First, the narrative flashes forward to the next winter when Rudy jumps into the freezing Amper River in order to retrieve a book for Liesel. The book is *The Whistler* which has not been mentioned up to this point prompting the questions: How did Liesel come by that book? And How did the book end up in the river? Second, the narrative flashes forward two years to Rudy's death during a bombing. Death makes "A SMALL ANNOUNCEMENT" about Rudy's undeserved death and the kiss that Liesel finally gives him. Of course, in the context of so much death at that stage of the war, the death of one small boy in an air raid could only be 'small'.

70. Explain Death's complex feelings about Rudy's death.

THE GAMBLERS (A SEVEN-SIDED DIE)

The narrative returns to mid-April 1941. Of course, a regular die can only have six sides, but when you gamble your whole future by concealing a Jew in your house you are playing with a seven sided die, and you cannot win the bet. Everything is going well until the seventh side of the dice shows up.

Max's waking dream of fighting Hitler has replaced his guilty nightmares. Liesel asks him who wins, and he says confidently that he does. It is "the words, the long cloud, and the figures on the wall" that give him the confidence of being victorious. Death comments, "It was as though he'd opened her palm, given her the words, and closed it up again." Symbolically, Max. Hans, Rosa and Liesel are painting over the words of *Mein Kampf*, obliterating their hateful message.

Liesel's ability to use words is illustrated. Her descriptions of the weather are precise yet poetical; they enable Max to envisage the world outside his basement. Her verbal abuse of Frau Hermann shows that she is no longer content to be a silent victim: it is "rich versus poor." In this conflict, for the first time in her life "it was Liesel who possessed the talking." However, Liesel uses words as the Nazis use them – to hurt and injure. She is shocked to see how much her words injure Ilsa; their effect is so powerful that Liesel imagines physical wounds, "Blood leaked from her nose and licked at her lips. Her eyes had blackened. Cuts had opened up ..." This is why Liesel thinks that she is going to hell.

71. Why is Liesel tempted to tell the Mayor's wife about Max?

72. Explain how Max's dream of boxing Hitler reflects the reality of being a Jew in Germany.

73. Compare and/or contrast Max's dream of fighting Hitler with Liesel's verbal attack on Ilsa Hermann.

74. Why does Liesel tell Rosa that she is responsible for the mayor stopping his laundry? Why doesn't Rosa give Liesel a beating?

RUDY'S YOUTH

Rudy's experience in the Hitler Youth is difficult because of Frank Deutscher, the sadistic leader. ('Deutscher' means 'German' so he symbolizes the Germans who fell under Hitler's influence.) He uses his power, officially conferred by the state, just as the adult Nazis, taking their cue from Hitler himself, use their power to oppress and humiliate the powerless. Rudy shares the same sense of loyalty to friends as both Hans and Liesel; like them, he will stick to his own moral code even when the consequence is punishment. Rudy, however, lacks Hans' prudence.

Rudy plays for pity but still does not get a kiss from Liesel. This is particularly sad because the reader knows that within two years he will be dead.

THE LOSERS

The new leader of the stealing gang, Viktor Chemmel, is the same sort of tyrant as Frank Deutscher. Both are mini-Hitlers using threats and brute force to impose their will. Both are obeyed unquestioningly, recalling the narrator's earlier question "what if the *other* is a lot more than one?" – what if one man can get a whole nation to follow him unthinkingly?

75. The chapter ends with ominous foreshadowing. How do you think that Viktor will get his revenge against Rudy?

SKETCHES

76. Explain Liesel's feelings when she sneaks a look at Max's sketches. Examine the double meaning of her statement, "You scared me, Max." (Clue: Max decides only to give Liesel the book when she is "old enough.")

THE WHISTLER AND THE SHOES

Having been humiliated once too often at the Hitler Youth, Rudy tells Liesel, "'I need a win, Liesel. Honestly.'" Though she is less aware of it, Liesel also needs a win because things have been getting progressively worse for her step-parents, so she vows to get her revenge on the mayor's wife who she feels has let her down. *The Whistler* is the third book that Liesel steals. This action marks the moment ("late October 1941") when she truly becomes "the book thief."

77. The mayor's wife offered to give Liesel the book *The Whistler*, but she refused it. Now she desperately wants to steal it. Explain the difference Liesel sees between getting the book as a gift and taking it.

THREE ACTS OF STUPIDITY BY RUDY STEINER

As Bakewell writes of life in German-occupied France, "Everyday life required constantly negotiating the balance between submission and resistance, as well as between ordinary activity and the extraordinary underlying reality" (*At the Existentialist Café* 144). Rudy's problem is that he lacks the sort of prudence that his own parents and Liesel's foster parents show.

78. Explain why the three things that Rudy does are *so* stupid. Why is Rudy taking risks?

THE FLOATING BOOK (Part II)

Liesel and Rudy continue to be persecuted by people in positions of power who embody Hitler's ideology, but Rudy finally achieves a victory by saving Liesel's copy of *The Whistler* from the river.

79. Why on earth doesn't Liesel give Rudy a kiss?

PART SIX: the dream carrier

DEATH'S DIARY: 1942

Death makes several references that may need explanation. AD 79 was the year in which Mount Vesuvius erupted burying the towns of Pompeii and Herculaneum and killing thousands. 1346 marked the beginning of the Black Death in Europe: fifty million people, 60% of Europe's entire population, died. Joseph Stalin's purges in Russia between 1936 and 1938 resulted in the execution of between half a million and one million people, with many more dying in famines. "THE ABRIDGED ROLL-CALL FOR 1942" refers to: the gas chambers and incinerators that were used for the extermination of Jews; Hitler's invasion of Russia, Operation Barbarossa, which led to the deaths of four million Russian soldiers; and to the Allied attack (August 19) on the coastal town of Dieppe, France, that resulted in nearly one thousand fatalities and many more wounded and taken prisoner.

Death finds relief from the strain of his job by remembering "the strewn pieces of beauty [he] saw in that time as well." Of these, the book thief provides the most memorable.

THE SNOWMAN

Liesel is Max's one connection with the outside world which she is continuously bringing into the basement. Like every other character, Liesel feels guilty for the suffering that she thinks she has caused Max by making the snowman. In a moment of typical grumbling, Rosa seems to agree, but Hans reminds her that the cause is something over which she has no control, "'Rosa, it started with Adolf.'"

80. Why does Liesel consider this the best Christmas ever?

81. When Liesel blames herself for Max's illness and asks her foster father, "'Why did I have to build that snowman?'", Hans replies, "'Liesel … you had to.'" Explain what you think he means.

THIRTEEN PRESENTS

Death remembers visiting Max, so he must have been on the point of dying. At the last minute, however, Max put up a fight to stay alive. Death was pleased to see it – he had plenty of work to do elsewhere. The tear that falls from Liesel's eye onto Max's face recalls the yellow tear that she cried earlier for her mother and foreshadows a tear she will shed later over Rudy's body.

FRESH AIR, AND OLD NIGHTMARE, AND WHAT TO DO WITH A JEWISH CORPSE

On the night of March 28-29, 1942, RAF Bomber Command attacked the medieval city of Lübeck, which became the first German city to go up in flames. On the night of May 30-31, the RAF launched its first 1,000 bomber raid on Cologne, resulting in just under five hundred killed. On October 30, the city of Munich was bombed. The tide of war had turned.

Liesel, with Rudy's help, steals another book from the mayor's house - *The Dream Carrier* which is about an abandoned child that wants to grow up to be a priest. Strangely, in winter, the window to the library is left open. The narrator suggests that it is left open deliberately to allow Liesel to gain access to the books. (Ilsa has, of course, noted the disappearance of *The Whistler*.) While Hans and Rosa talk about what they could possibly do to dispose of Max's body should he die, Liesel is adamant that he is not dead yet. Having been supported so many times by her foster parents, it is now her turn to support them.

Liesel fulfills her role as *The Standover* Man; she also gives Max the gift of words in her written description of the monster cloud and by reading to him both when he is unconscious and when he finally wakes up to prevent him from falling back into the deep sleep of a coma. Max has become a surrogate for Liesel's dead brother: she was helpless when her brother died, but she is not helpless now and determines to fight for Max's life. Ironically, as Max's health improves, the situation in Germany gets worse as a result of increased Allied bombing raids.

82. How would you interpret the dream that Liesel has of Max replacing her brother?

"Death's Diary: Cologne"

Notice how the narrative concentrates on colors. Amid so much dying, the narrator seeks out his normal distraction.

83. What more does the reader learn about Death's attitude to his vocation?

THE VISITOR

Liesel's quick thinking saves the life of Max and probably also of Hans and Rosa.

84. Why does Max feel the need to apologize at the end of the chapter?

THE SCHUNZELER

Liesel is very relieved to have evaded detection, but Rudy senses her fear and guilt, though he cannot identify its true cause. Liesel's confident assertion, "'Everything's good'" reflects her relief that Max avoided capture and pride in her own part in making sure that he did. It is, however, an example of dramatic irony, for as the narrator tells us unknown to Liesel, "Things were on the verge of decay."

DEATH'S DIARY: THE PARISIANS

Between June 1940 and January 1945, an estimated 1.3 million people arrived at Auschwitz in Poland. 1.1 million of them died in the gas chambers there, including over 900,000 Jews. The first trainloads of Jews from Paris arrived at Auschwitz on March 30, 1942. Death claims "the sky was the color of Jews." This is because of the smoke from the crematoria in the concentration camps where the bodies of poisoned Jews were burned. Death imagines the sky past that, "knowing without question that the sun was blond, and the endless atmosphere was a giant blue eye." This symbolically suggests that the Jews are killed because of the racial theories of the Nazis. Even Death has no more insight into God than ordinary humans do and the question 'Why did God let it happen?' burns as much for him as it does for the reader.

85. The reader is given even greater insight into the narrator's feelings about his eternal task. How does what Death says affect your feelings for this character?

86. Explain the narrator's final statement, "… they were you."

PART SEVEN: the complete duden dictionary and thesaurus

CHAMPAIGNE AND ACCORDIAN

In the summer of 1942, the people of Molching are waiting for the inevitable air raids.

87. The time that Liesel spends with Hans is "the best time of her life." Explain what makes it so.

88. Comment on the narrator's use of the simile, "Hard times were coming. Like a parade."?

THE TRILOGY

Liesel steals a third novel from the mayor's home. It is titled *A Song in the Dark* and has a green cover. She does this alone, but a week later, with Rudy, Liesel sees a book that has been placed on the outside of on a closed window. Liesel *The Complete Duden Dictionary and Thesaurus* in which Rudy finds a letter of apology from Ilsa to Liesel.

Rudy and Liesel ride home "from summer to autumn," foreshadowing the end of their happiness.

89. Why do you think Rudy intentionally disqualifies himself from the 100 m race?

90. Having gone back to the mayor's house but failed to knock on the front door, Liesel consider herself to be a criminal. Explain why?

THE SOUND OF SIRENS

Death feels sympathy for the individuals in the shelter. They do not deserve their fate – particularly the children. However, he feels more sympathy for the Jews taken to the 'showers' because they had no chance of living whereas the people in the basement do, "For those people life was still achievable." Max admits that during the air raid he looked outside. He was taking a very small risk because he had not seen the outside world for twenty-two months.

THE SKY STEALER

In the shelter during the second air raid, Liesel learns the power of words. She reads from chapter one of *The Whistler*, and soon everyone is listening intently to her. (The scene is obviously a contrast to the disaster in the classroom when Liesel tried to do a reading test.) The narrator writes, "she hauled the words in and breathed them out. A voice played the notes inside her. This, it said, is your accordion." Thus far, Liesel's experience of words (both the words of others and of herself) has been largely restricted to hateful and coercive language, but she now discovers that she has the power to use words to soothe and comfort. Rosa is particularly proud of her. Max is inspired by the story to begin writing *The Word Shaker*.

FRAU HOLTZAPFEL'S OFFER

91. The statement that the Jews marched through Molching "were going to Dachau to concentrate" is the narrator's joke. What point is Death making?

THE LONG WALK TO DACHAU

The soldiers decide to parade the Jews through Molching on their way to Dachau. The Jewish prisoners are exhausted, starving, and many are near death showing the terrible cruelty of the Nazi soldiers and of those citizens who support them. Hans is the only person moved to pity by what he sees: his humanity causes him to offer a starving old man a small piece of bread – just as earlier he had painted out racist slurs on the doors of Jews. For this act, Hans is whipped by one of the soldiers. (On the night of the book-burning, when Liesel shouts out "'I hate the Führer'" Hans slaps Liesel across the face and tells her, "'You can say that in our house … But you never say it on the street, at school, at the BDM, never!'" It is easier for Hans to give rules about separating private and public conduct than it is for him to control his own behavior to conform to those rules.)

92. Why does Hans eventually decide to let Liesel witness the Jews passing thorough Molching on their way to Dachau?

93. What are the immediate consequences of Hans' act of humanity? What are the future consequences that he fears?

PEACE

When Hans' tells Max what he has done and that he expects to be arrested and his house searched that very night, Max leaves – he has no alternative. Now it is Hans' turn to feel guilty. Max agrees to meet Hans four days later by the broken bridge across the Amper, but he will not keep their appointment.

94. Explain the meaning of the note Hans finds at the river.

95. Why do you think that Death does not equate the word "silence" with the synonyms *"quiet, calmness, peace"*?

THE IDIOT AND THE COAT MEN

Ironically, Hans is not arrested for offering comfort to the Jewish prisoner. This makes him feel even more guilty because he has caused Max to leave a safe hiding place when there was actually no reason for Max to go. He feels that he *ought* to be punished. Liesel now reassures Hans that he did nothing wrong (as earlier he had reassured her). It is also Liesel who identifies the coat men as Gestapo, the State Secret Police (Geheime Staatspolizei).

The reader might guess why they are visiting the Steiners' house: recall this statement about Rudy's performance on the sports' day, "*** **A POINT FOR FUTURE REFERENCE *** Not only was Rudy recognized now as a good school student. He was a gifted athlete, too.**"

PART EIGHT: the word shaker

DOMINOES AND DARKNESS

The fallen dominoes symbolize the lives of people who become victims of the war. Death uses his/her knowledge of the future to point to the tragic irony that while Barbara and Alex Steiner act to protect Rudy by refusing to allow him to go to a school for elite Nazis, their decision unwittingly contributes to his death later in the story.

THE THOUGHT OF RUDY NAKED

There is a flashback to the physical examination that Rudy and two other boys had at school the aim of which was to find recruits for what the nurse called "'a new class of physically and mentally advanced Germans. An officer class.'" Rudy and one other boy had been selected. The scene is quite comic given the embarrassment of the boys and the terrible cold that the doctor has.

96. In what way does the incident of the physical examination which Rudy describes to Liesel mark an important change in her feelings for her friend?

PUNISHMENT

In November 1942, Alex Steiner and Hans are both called up to serve in the army: it is their punishment for each having defied the Party (one by refusing to give up his son and the other by helping a starving Jew) – or, at least, this is how they see it. Once again, language is being used to hurt; Liesel notes that "The words had been punched forcefully into the paper … Words like *compulsory* and *duty* were beaten into the page." The impact of the words is seen on Rosa's face down which Liesel describes a tear falling.

PROMISE KEEPER'S WIFE

First Hans and then, four days after, Alex leave Himmel Street and nothing is quite the same without them. Both Liesel and Rudy are grieving, but as she tells Rudy, "'you've only lost your father'" – a remark that he does not understand.

Rudy's desire to kill the Führer is typical of his romantic but impractical nature.

97. With Hans gone, the focus falls on Rosa. How is she affected by the absence of her husband?

THE COLLECTOR

While Alex Steiner repairs uniforms in Vienna, Hans is sent to Essen to join the LSE, the Air Raid Special Unit – a dangerous job because they have to stay above ground during air raids and try to minimize the damage. After the raids, Hans encounters the dead, a heart-breaking experience for such a loving man, and even worse are the people who emerge from the wreckage, calling out names of the missing. One man dies in Hans' arms and he trips over the corpse of an eleven- or twelve-year-old boy whose name, ironically, proves to be Rudy. In many ways, Hans' role is similar to that of Death, which is why the narrator comments that Hans will "need to perfect the art of forgetting."

98. Explain why the letter that Hans writes home is so short.

THE BREAD EATERS

Liesel attends the parades of Jews looking to see if Max is among them. If he is, she will know that he is alive (though for how long), but if he is not she will know he has not yet been caught. It is an impossible position. Rudy's rebellion against the Nazis has taken a more practical and a more moral direction, under the influence of Liesel's step father, Hans.

THE HIDDEN SKETCHBOOK

When there is another air raid, Liesel reads to the people huddled fearfully in the shelter, and they find comfort in it. Rosa decides that Liesel is now ready for the gift that Max left her: she tells Liesel, "'I think you have always been ready.'"

The Word Shaker is an allegory which essentially encapsulates the meaning of *The Book Thief*. It tells the story of the friendship between Max and Liesel, but also how Hitler exploited the power of words to generate hatred in the people. Hitler's allies were the word shakers (perhaps representing members of the Nazi Party) who shook down words of hatred from the trees to generate a whole forest of hatred (representing the Nazi ideology). Then, a skinny girl (Liesel) lets fall a tear of sympathy over "a man who was despised by her homeland" (Max). The result is a seed which the girl plants. It grows into a huge tree, because kindness and humanity will always overcome hatred, and the girl protects it from all of Hitler's efforts to chop it down. Even when the tree falls, its trunk provides a path through the forest of hateful words on which the girl and boy escape hearing behind them other voices of kindness and humanity. This, one act of compassion has begun the destruction of Hitler's tyranny.

99. Why does Rosa decide to give Liesel Max's book at this particular moment?

THE ANARCHIST'S SUIT COLLECTION

Liesel obtains Rudy's Christmas gift from his father's closed-up shop. When Rudy falls and admits that he misses his father, the narrator urges, "'Kiss him, Liesel, kiss him,'" but she does not.

100. Explain why Death urges Liesel to kiss the fallen Rudy, even though he/she knows that she will not do so.

PART NINE: the last human stranger

THE NEXT TEMPTATION

The last book the Liesel steals from the library is *The Last Human Stranger*.

101. When Liesel finds stale cookies waiting for her in the library of the mayor's house it occurs to her that either the mayor knows about her thieving visits or the library belongs to Ilsa Hermann, not to her husband. This idea (soon confirmed when the mayor's wife appears in the library) is very important to Liesel. Explain why.

THE CARDPLAYER

Reinhold Zucker, a young man in Hans' unit, is soon going to die in Hans' place as a result of a trivial argument.

102. The narrator ends the chapter by saying, "It kills me sometimes, how people die." There is a play on words here, but is Death making a joke or is he/she deadly serious? Explain your answer.

THE SNOWS OFF STALINGRAD

When Liesel goes to Frau Holtzapfel's for her normal reading, the door is opened by her son Michael, though he is so changed that Liesel does not recognize him. Michael, who has been injured, has brought his mother the news that his brother, Robert, has been killed at Stalingrad. The war has its first victims in Himmel Street. Liesel shows her bravery and selflessness in going to read to the bereaved mother – a woman who has for so long behaved hatefully toward the Hubermanns.

103. The narrator writes, "The sky was white but deteriorating fast. As always, it was becoming an enormous drop sheet. Blood was bleeding through, and in patches the clouds were dirty, like footprints in melting snow. Footprints? you ask. Well, I wonder whose those could be." What do you think he/she means?

THE AGELESS BROTHER

Liesel takes back to 8 Grande Strasse the plate which she stole with the cookies. She imagines her six-year-old brother approving of the action. Finally, Liesel is able to accept his death, and he no longer invades her dreams. Like everyone else she has known and loved, he appears to Liesel in her waking imagination.

THE ACCIDENT

The thing about dying is how arbitrary it is. There is no logic to it and certainly no fairness. In being sent home, Hans is considered lucky by his sergeant, but Hans will be killed because he was sent home.

104. Zucker is killed when the LSE truck rolls over because he has insisted on sitting in Hans's seat.

What past incident in Hans' life does his escape recall?

THE BITTER TASTE OF QUESTION

105. Explain Rudy's response when Liesel tells him about the letter she and Rosa have received from Papa.

ONE TOOLBOX, ONE BLENDER, ONE BEAR

Rudy's thieving excursion is another of his futile attempts to get his revenge against the Nazi regime that has brought his family, and Germany, so much apparently random suffering. He aims to steal from the rich Nazis who seem immune to the suffering they have caused. In this way he feels that he will restore some fairness to the world.

The bombing of Munich described in this chapter took place on March 9, 1943. Approximately 260 RAF bombers attacked the city in which 208 people were killed and 425 injured. Michael Holtzapfel fails to persuade his mother to take shelter from the air raid. Like many other characters in the novel, he feels guilty about being alive and wanting to stay alive when his brother is dead, and now his mother wants to die. Michael feels the same guilt about leaving her and going to the shelter as did Max when he left his family on Kristallnacht (November 9 to November 10, 1938). Michael does not understand, "'... how she [his mother] can sit there ready to die while I still want to live ... Why do I want to live? I shouldn't want to, but I do.'"

Fortunately, Liesel has "a multitude of words and sentences ... at her fingertips." The word shaker is able to use her words to get Frau Holtzapfel to move to the shelter, despite the fact that her words are almost drowned out by the bombs.

When Rudy finds the dying enemy pilot, he makes a gesture of humanity that impresses Death. The narrator continues to be fascinated by the paradoxical nature of humans who are capable of so much that is ugly but also of so much that is beautiful. (In contrast, Death's psychology lacks this complexity: he is, as it were, programmed to perform one action and to do it to the best of his ability each time.)

106. Explain why, despite his intentions, "Rudy Steiner wasn't stealing anything" from the houses of the rich Nazis.

107. Look closely at the final paragraph in this chapter. In what ways does Death feel him/herself to be different from humans? How does Death feel about these differences?

HOMECOMING

As often, in the final sentence, the narrator foreshadows the coming tragedy for Liesel.

PART TEN: the book thief
THE END OF THE WORLD (Part 1)

In a flash forward, the narrator tells the reader of the terrible fate of everyone on Himmel Street – everyone except Liesel. Like so many others, these deaths are purely random, the result of "off target" bombs. Liesel's life is protected, quite literally, by her love of words.

108. Explain the final sentence of the chapter, "[Liesel] was holding desperately on to the words who had saved her life."

THE NINETY EIGHT DAY

As conditions get worse, Jewish prisoners are brought into the town to help with the clean-up following raids. The narrator speculates that as the citizens blame the Jews for their misfortune they should also "have blamed the *Führer* and his quest for Russia as the actual cause," though there is no sign that they actually do so. Michael Holtzapfel commits suicide because of his feelings of guilt. Paradoxically, "He killed himself for wanting to live." Metaphorically, the snow of Stalingrad extends into Frau Holtzapfel's kitchen.

109. Death describes Michael Holtzapfel on July 24th as "Another human pendulum. Another clock, stopped." What is the narrator trying to convey by this metaphor?

THE WAR MAKER

In the last week of July 1943, the Allies conducted a series of air raids on Hamburg in what was termed Operation Gomorrah – a systematic attempt to destroy the city. It was on 27 July that most of 42,600 civilians died. Ten square miles of the city were obliterated, and 900,000 of its inhabitants forced to flee. The situation in Germany is getting worse, but Hitler continues to make war. Death comments, "He certainly had an iron will."

WAY OF THE WORDS

Liesel identifies Max in the parade of Jews through the town. Just as her foster father had once done, she rushes to the aid of a Jew in total disregard of the consequent punishment she will receive. Each time Jews have been brought through, she has looked for him, and as the Jews are paraded through town, Max is the only one looking out, searching the faces of the civilians for Liesel.

110. On the reason for marching more Jews toward Dachau, the narrator comments, "It was possible that more work needed to be done in the camp, or several prisoners had died." Comment on the tone of this remark. (Clue: Death knows very well why Jews were being taken to Dachau, and so does any reader with a smattering of historical knowledge.)

111. Explain why Liesel reminds Max of the "strange, small man" and "the word shaker."

112. How does Rudy try to protect Liesel? How does she react? How does the narrator react?

113. Explain the title of this chapter. (Clue: Think back to the story *The Word Shaker*, particularly the final image of the fallen tree.)

CONFESSIONS

The theme of missed opportunities appears strongly in this short chapter. In this case, there are words that Liesel does not say and desires that she does not communicate to Rudy. Unlike the narrator and the reader, Liesel does not realize that she is missing her last chance.

114. In what ways are Liesel and Rudy shown to be closer than they have ever been before.

ILSA HERMANN'S LITTLE BLACK BOOK

Liesel goes back to the library, but she becomes obsessed by the destructive power of words and in revenge tears a book to shreds. However, she leaves a letter for Frau Hermann in which, without being conscious of it, she shows the positive power of words. Frau Hermann comes to visit Liesel at 33 Himmel Street to give her a notebook in which to write her own words: having been saved from despair by Liesel, Ilsa now performs that function for the girl. It is the story Liesel wrote that Death has picked up and which he has carried with him everywhere.

THE RIB CAGE PLANES

115. On page 42 of her story, Liesel uses a metaphor to describe Papa. Why is the comparison appropriate?

THE END OF THE WORLD (Part II)

This is a very sad chapter: so many dead; so many things not said and done that now can never be said and done. In particular, Liesel regrets that she never kissed Rudy because she now realizes that she loved him all along, and she regrets the things that she never told Mama even though she knew all along that Mama loved both her and Papa but could only express her love in harsh words.

116. How is it possible for Death to tell the story of the Book Thief? Why is Death telling the story of the Book Thief? (Clue: Death becomes a book thief and in writing his/her own story also becomes a word shaker.)

EPILOGUE: the last color

DEATH AND LIESEL

In a flash forward, the narrator describes Liesel's death "only yesterday" having lived "to a very old age."

WOOD IN THE AFTERNOON

Ilsa Hermann has saved Liesel from despair by showing her the positive power of words. It was her gift of a blank notebook that saved Liesel's life, and in this chapter she gives Liesel a home. At the same time, of course, Liesel replaces Isla's dead son and in so doing helps to make Isla whole again.

Liesel refusal to wash the dirt of the Himmel Street bombing from her body recalls her similar refusal to take a bath when she first came to the Hubermanns' house. Tragedies such as she has experienced remain with one for a lifetime.

Death describes how Liesel describes the sky at the time she told Alex Steiner how Rudy died, "In Liesel's vision, the sky I saw was gray and glossy. A silver afternoon." This recalls the silver eyes of Hans Hubermann: Liesel is acting with the humanity that he taught her. Like many others in the story, Alex Steiner has regrets: had he simply allowed Rudy to go to the Nazi school, his son would still have been alive.

MAX

Liesel sees Max again after the liberation of Dachau, but the narrator tells us nothing of their future relationship.

THE HANDOVER MAN

117. Explain the title of this chapter.

118. Explain why Death is "**haunted by humans**."

Post-Reading Activities:

1. Create a hypothetical map of Molching based on the descriptions in the text and indicate by annotation the locations of the main events in the novel.

2. Liesel would have been born in January or February, 1930. This means that, at the time I am writing this, she would be approximately eighty-six years and eight months old. (That's quite old, of course, but Liesel might live until 2026 or even beyond.) Imagine you are a student (you decide what level from elementary school to college level) in Sydney, Australia, given a project to interview a survivor of the Second World War. What questions would you ask Liesel and how would she answer? Produce your interview either in the form of a written transcript only, or a transcript and audio, or even (if you can find someone willing to play the part of Liesel) as a transcript and video. This could be a group project.

3. Research the case of John Demjanjuk, an elderly former Ohio car worker born in Ukraine who was finally convicted of Nazi war crimes. Present the case either for the prosecution or the defense (depending on the conclusions you reach in your research).

Guide to Further Reading

Elie Wiesel's *Night* (1960) is the autobiographical account of a young Jewish boy caught up in Hitler's "Final Solution." It covers the on-set of persecution right up to the liberation of those still alive in the camps.

The Annex: Diary Notes 14 June 1942 – 1 August 1944 (1947) is better known as ***The Diary of a Young Girl*** or ***The Diary of Anne Frank***. If you are going to read it (and you *should*), then make sure that you get a modern, uncensored text. For decades editors thought it was their job to present Anne Frank as some sort of saint so they took out all references to her (perfectly normal) sexual feelings.

M. E. Kerr's *Gentlehands* (1978) is a Young Adult novel about the protagonist's grandfather who is suddenly accused of having been a brutal SS guard at Auschwitz.

Bibliography

Blasdel, Janelle. *CliffsNotes on "The Book Thief"*. 11 Sep 2016

Justin T. Cass. Chazelle, Damien ed. *"The Book Thief" Study Guide*. GradeSaver, 30 November 2009 Web. 11 September 2016.

SparkNotes Editors. *SparkNote on "The Book Thief"*. SparkNotes.com. SparkNotes LLC. 2013. Web. 15 Aug. 2016.

Ydstie, John. "Call Me Death: Odd Narrator of a Girl's Story." *npr books*. National Public Radio, 2 Apr. 2006. Web. 14 Sept. 2016.

Appendix 1: Literary Terms relevant to this text

Allusion: a passing, brief or indirect reference to a well known person or place, or to something of historical, cultural, literary or political importance.

Ambiguous, ambiguity: when a statement is unclear in meaning – ambiguity may be deliberate or accidental.

Analogy: a comparison which treats two things as identical in one or more specified ways (e.g., "What's in a name? That which we call a rose / By any other word would smell as sweet" [Juliet in *Romeo and Juliet*].

Antagonist: a character or force opposing the protagonist.

Antithesis: the complete opposite of something (e.g., "Use every man after his *desert*, and who should 'scape *whipping?*" [Hamlet in *Hamlet*]).

Authorial comment: when the writer addresses the reader directly (not to be confused with the narrator doing so).

Climax: the conflict to which the action has been building since the start of the play or story.

Comic inversion: reversing the normally accepted order of language or of things for comic effect.

Connotation: the ideas, feelings and associations generated by a word or phrase or with an object or animal.

Dialogue: a conversation between two or more people in direct speech.

Diction: the writer's choice of particular words (the use of vocabulary) in order to create a particular effect.

First person: first person singular is "I" and plural is "we".

Foreshadowing: a statement or action which gives the reader a hint of what is likely to happen later in the narrative.

Genre: the type of literature into which a particular text falls (e.g. drama, poetry, novel).

Image, imagery: figurative language such as simile, metaphor, personification etc., or a description which conjures up a particularly vivid picture.

Imply, implication: when the text suggests to the reader a meaning which it does not actually state.

Infer, inference: the reader's act of going beyond what is stated in the text to draw conclusions.

Irony, ironic: a form of humor which undercuts the apparent meaning of a statement:

Conscious irony: irony used deliberately by a writer or character;

Unconscious irony: a statement or action which has significance for the reader of which the character is unaware;

Dramatic irony: when an action has an important significance that is obvious to the reader but not to one or more of the characters;

Tragic irony: when a character says (or does) something which will have a serious, even fatal, consequence for him/ her. The audience is aware of the error, but the character is not;

Verbal irony: the conscious use of particular words which are appropriate to what is being said.

Image, imagery: figurative language such as simile, metaphor, personification etc., or a description which conjures up a particularly vivid picture.

Imply / implication: when the text suggests to the reader a meaning which it does not actually state.

Infer/ inference: the reader's act of going beyond what is stated in the text to draw conclusions.

Irony, ironic: a form of humor which undercuts the apparent meaning of a statement (e.g., Cassius is being ironic when he says of Julius Caesar, "'tis true this god did shake" [*Julius Caesar*]).

Juxtaposition: literally putting two things side by side for purposes of comparison and/ or contrast.

Literal: the surface level of meaning that a statement has.

Metaphor / metaphorical: the description of one thing by direct comparison with another (e.g. the coal-black night).

Extended metaphor: a comparison which is developed at length.

Motif: a frequently repeated idea, image or situation in a text.

Motivation: why a character acts as he/she does – in modern literature motivation is seen as psychological.

Narrator / Narrative voice: the voice that the reader hears in the text – not to be confused with the author.

Perspective: point of view from which a story, or an incident within a story, is told.

Personified / personification: a simile or metaphor in which an inanimate object or abstract idea is described by comparison with a human.

Plot: a chain of events linked by cause and effect.

Prologue: an introduction which gives a lead-in to the main story.

Protagonist: the character who initiates the action and is most likely to have the sympathy of the audience.

Realism: a text that describes the action in a way that appears to reflect life.

Setting: the environment in which the narrative (or part of the narrative) takes place.

Simile: a description of one thing by explicit comparison with another (e.g., "My love is like a red, red rose" [Burns]).

Extended simile: a comparison which is developed at length.

Style: the way in which a writer chooses to express him/ herself. Style is a vital aspect of meaning since how something is expressed can crucially affect what is being written or spoken.

Suspense: the building of tension in the reader.

Symbol, symbolic, symbolism, symbolize: a physical object which comes to represent an abstract idea (e.g. the sun may symbolize life).

Themes: important concepts, beliefs and ideas explored and presented in a text.

Third person: third person singular is "he/ she/ it" and plural is "they" – authors often write novels in the third person.

Tone: literally the sound of a text – how words sound (either in the mouth of an actor or the head of a reader) can crucially affect meaning.

Literary terms activity

As you use each term in the study guide, fill in the definition of the term and include an example from the text to show how it is used.

The first definition is supplied. Find an example in the text to complete it.

Term	Definition
	Example
foreshadow	*a statement or action which gives the reader a hint of what is likely to happen later in the narrative*
genre	
implied, imply, implication	
irony, ironic	
paradox, paradoxical	
symbol, symbolic, symbolism, symbolize	
theme	

Plot graph

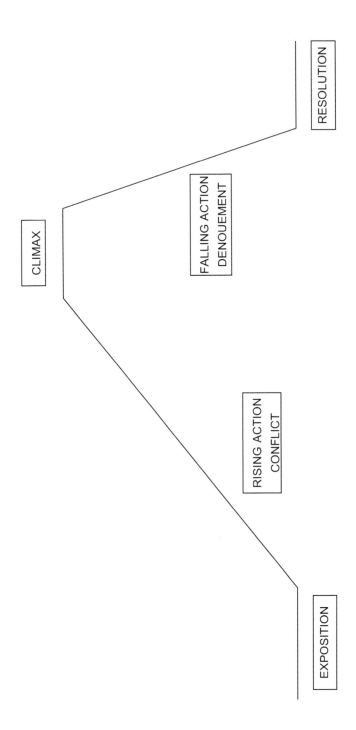

Different perspectives on the situation that initiates action in the novel

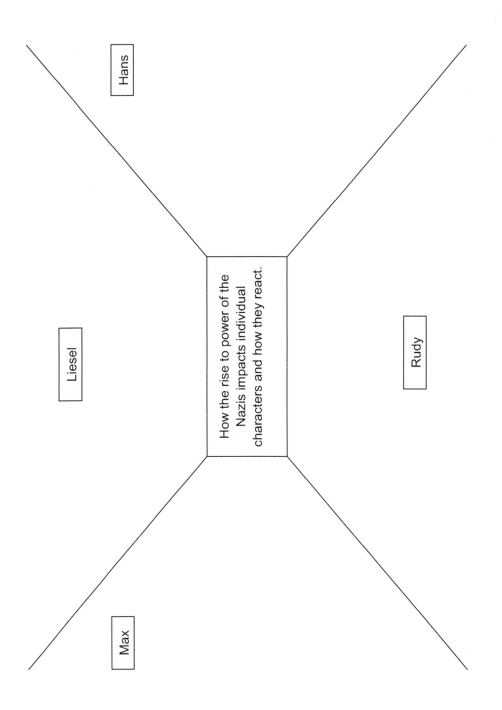

Appendix 2: How I Used the Study Guide Questions

Although there are both closed and open questions in the Study Guide, very few of them have simple, right or wrong answers. They are designed to encourage in-depth discussion, disagreement, and (eventually) consensus. Above all, they aim to encourage students to go to the text to support their conclusions and interpretations.

I am not so arrogant as to presume to tell teachers how they should use this resource. I used it in the following ways, each of which ensured that students were well prepared for class discussion and presentations.

1. Set a reading assignment for the class and tell everyone to be aware that the questions will be the focus of whole class discussion the next class.

2. Set a reading assignment for the class and allocate particular questions to sections of the class (e.g. if there are four questions, divide the class into four sections, etc.).

In class, form discussion groups containing one person who has prepared each question and allow time for feedback within the groups.

Have feedback to the whole class on each question by picking a group at random to present their answers and to follow up with class discussion.

3. Set a reading assignment for the class, but do not allocate questions.

In class, divide students into groups and allocate to each group one of the questions related to the reading assignment the answer to which they will have to present formally to the class.

Allow time for discussion and preparation.

4. Set a reading assignment for the class, but do not allocate questions.

In class, divide students into groups and allocate to each group one of the questions related to the reading assignment.

Allow time for discussion and preparation.

Now reconfigure the groups so that each group contains at least one person who has prepared each question and allow time for feedback within the groups.

5. Before starting to read the text, allocate specific questions to individuals or pairs. (It is best not to allocate all questions to allow for other approaches and variety. One in three questions or one in four seems about right.) Tell students that they will be leading the class discussion on their question. They will need to start with a brief presentation of the issues and then conduct a question and answer session. After this, they will be expected to present a brief review of the discussion.

6. Having finished the text, arrange the class into groups of 3, 4 or 5. Tell each group to select as many questions from the Study Guide as there are members of the group.

Each individual is responsible for drafting out a written answer to one question, and each answer should be a substantial paragraph.

Each group as a whole is then responsible for discussing, editing and suggesting improvements to each answer, which is revised by the original writer and brought back to the group for a final proof reading followed by revision.

This seems to work best when the group knows that at least some of the points for the activity will be based on the quality of all of the answers.

To the Reader

Ray strives to make his products the best that they can be. If you have any comments or questions about this book *please* contact the author through his email: **moore.ray1@yahoo.com**
Visit his website at **http://www.raymooreauthor.com**
Also by Ray Moore: Most books are available from amazon.com as paperbacks and at most online eBook retailers.

Fiction:

The Lyle Thorne Mysteries: each book features five tales from the Golden Age of Detection:

Investigations of The Reverend Lyle Thorne
Further Investigations of The Reverend Lyle Thorne
Early Investigations of Lyle Thorne
Sanditon Investigations of The Reverend Lyle Thorne
Final Investigations of The Reverend Lyle Thorne
Lost Investigations of The Reverend Lyle Thorne

Non-fiction:

The ***Critical Introduction series*** is written for high school teachers and students and for college undergraduates. Each volume gives an in-depth analysis of a key text:

"The Stranger" by Albert Camus: A Critical Introduction (Revised Second Edition)
"The General Prologue" by Geoffrey Chaucer: A Critical Introduction
"Pride and Prejudice" by Jane Austen: A Critical Introduction
"The Great Gatsby" by F. Scott Fitzgerald: A Critical Introduction

The Text and Critical Introduction series differs from the Critical introduction series as these books contain the original text and in the case of the medieval texts an interlinear translation to aid the understanding of the text. The commentary allows the reader to develop a deeper understanding of the text and themes within the text.

"Sir Gawain and the Green Knight": Text and Critical Introduction
"The General Prologue" by Geoffrey Chaucer: Text and Critical Introduction
"The Wife of Bath's Prologue and Tale" by Geoffrey Chaucer: Text and Critical Introduction
"Heart of Darkness" by Joseph Conrad: Text and Critical Introduction
"The Sign of Four" by Sir Arthur Conan Doyle Text and Critical Introduction
"A Room with a View" By E.M. Forster: Text and Critical Introduction
"Oedipus Rex" by Sophocles: Text and Critical Introduction
"Henry V" by William Shakespeare: Text and Critical Introduction

Study guides available in print - listed alphabetically by author

* denotes also available as an eBook
"ME and EARL and the Dying GIRL" by Jesse Andrews: A Study Guide
"Wuthering Heights" by Emily Brontë: A Study Guide *
"Jane Eyre" by Charlotte Brontë: A Study Guide *

A Study Guide

Study Guides available as e-books:
New titles are added regularly.

Teacher resources:
Ray also publishes many more study guides and other resources for classroom use on the 'Teachers Pay Teachers' website:
http://www.teacherspayteachers.com/Store/Raymond-Moore

81945418R00038

Made in the USA
Middletown, DE
30 July 2018